Especially for

_____

From

_____

Date

_____

Published by Barbour Publishing, Inc., P.O. Box 719, Uhrichsville, Ohio 44683, www.barbourbooks.com

Our mission is to publish and distribute inspirational products offering exceptional value and biblical encouragement to the masses.

Member of the
Evangelical Christian
Publishers Association

Printed in China.

Simple Tips for
Simple Living

BARBOUR
PUBLISHING

The Best Things in Life Are Nearest:

Breath in your nostrils, light in your eyes,
flowers at your feet, duties at your hand,
the path of right just before you.
Then do not grasp at the stars, but do life's
plain, common work as it comes, certain
that daily duties and daily bread are
the sweetest things in life.
ROBERT LOUIS STEVENSON

Know Why

Have a clear reason for why each activity you do is important. Things we do just to please or impress someone else cause us the most stress and should be eliminated.

Spend Wisely

Buy only what you need and
can afford without going into debt.

Open Windows

Use fans and open windows more days in the year than you use the air conditioner—and welcome the outside sounds and smells indoors. Even a house needs to breathe sometimes.

Listen

The time you take to stop and really listen to your family and friends is never wasted time.

Morning Prayers
Prayers in the morning start each day on the right path.

Bedtime Prayers

Prayers at night help the mind and body relax.

Write a Letter

Handwrite a letter and mail it with a stamp.
Seems old-fashioned and slow, but your words will
come across as more meaningful. And consider how
personal a handwritten letter can be.
It truly is one of a kind.

{

Happiness

It is not how much we have, but how much we enjoy, that makes happiness.
CHARLES H. SPURGEON

}

Eat In

Make eating at home your first choice. It easily saves money, but it also brings a family closer as the family works together on preparing the meal and shares it around the table. Besides, leftovers for lunch the next day are a healthy and economical alternative to fast food or cafeteria food.

Real Treasure

"Do not store up for yourselves treasures on earth, where moth and rust destroy, and where thieves break in and steal. But store up for yourselves treasures in heaven, where moth and rust do not destroy, and where thieves do not break in and steal. For where your treasure is, there your heart will be also."

MATTHEW 6:19–21 NIV

Sabbath Rest

Take a Sabbath day (or at least a block of several hours) once a week. This day lets the body and mind fully rest and is a good time for recharging the spirit, too.

{

"No" Can be a Good Word

Learn to say "no" to things you don't
like doing or that aren't necessary.
Don't act out of obligation or guilt.

}

Less Is More—Possessions

It has been said that we can become a slave to our possessions. The more we own, the more we have to take care of in storing, cleaning, fixing, replacing, and more. Consider how having less stuff will actually free your time, money, and worries.

Importance of Community

Foster a community of friends and family;
then share your skills and abilities.

Debt Busters

Extra money from bonuses, tax returns, rebates, and gifts should go toward paying off debt before spending on entertainment and pleasure items.

Boundaries and Rules

Create boundaries in which your kids
can live and thrive. But keep family
rules simple and consistent.

Do It Yourself
Don't buy something you can make yourself and don't pay for someone to fix something you can learn to fix yourself.

Game Night

Have family game night at least once a week.

Buy Old

Shop antique stores, yard sales, and flea markets when you need something. Old things were made better than today's disposable plastic and may still have a lot of life left in them.

{
Committed to Family

Reduce the number of commitments you
make outside the family circle.
The commitment to raising a family is the
most important one you can make.
}

Always Grateful
When you adopt an attitude of thankfulness for all you have—even the unpleasant things—then your life will reflect peace and tranquility.

Alone but Not Lonely

Be sure to get a daily dose of alone time.
Time to think. Time to not think.
Time to pray. Time to unwind.

Errand Day

Time equals money, so combine errands
into one day and save on trips.

Ask for Help

There is no need to be a Lone Ranger.
It's okay to ask someone to help you complete
a project, learn a new skill, or whatever it may
be. Most people around us are not aware of
our need until we ask for help.

Discipline

He who heeds discipline shows the way to life,
but whoever ignores correction leads others astray.

PROVERBS 10:17 NIV

Take Care of Yourself

Treat your body with respect, giving it healthy food, rest, and exercise. In return, your body will take care of you for many productive years.

Information Download

Limit your exposure to media—TV, radio, news sources, advertisements, and Internet. Especially avoid information overload on topics that need not affect your sphere of life.

{

Judge Not

Don't worry about your neighbor or judge
others' actions. Each day has enough
stresses without your adding others'
problems to your own.

}

Do the Opposite

Recognize that often doing what is opposite from pop culture will make us the most happy and at peace with ourselves and our Lord.

Less Is More—Career

The higher up on the corporate ladder and the higher your salary, the more time and energy the job will take from you and your family. And the higher the job takes you into social circles, the more money you will usually end up spending on clothing, housing, and entertainment. Consider making a job downsize, as less responsibility and less income can equal more time, less stress, and less expenses.

Be Patient

Know that there are few times we can actually
change things or hurry things along.
So learn to be patient in the meantime and use the
waiting periods to relax and reflect.
The time for rushing will return soon enough.

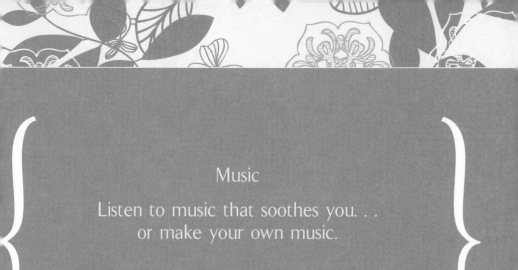

Music

Listen to music that soothes you. . .
or make your own music.

Be Deliberate

Be deliberate in your activities, paying full attention to the task at hand. You will get the most out of each life experience, retain more memories, and be more relaxed.

Mini-Vacations

Plan three or four local mini-vacations each year instead of one elaborate trip requiring heavy travel time and expense.

One Menu

Make the rule that the whole family eats the
same meal. Teach children to respect
the cook and try new foods.

Hospitality

Have a guest room (or a plan) always ready to receive a visitor or a friend in need. Hospitality is an often overlooked act of love.

Pray Together

Set aside time for family prayer, and let your children and spouse hear you lift their names before God.

Stick to the Basics

Buy only the basics within your budget. Have the kids save their own money to purchase brand names or other wants outside the family budget.

Clotheslines

Use a clothesline on laundry day. There is nothing quite like the smell of clothes dried in the out-of-doors. Also, the sun has a way of taking care of bacteria that the washer and dryer can't.

{

Leave a Legacy

A good man leaves an inheritance
for his children's children.
PROVERBS 13:22 NIV

}

Use It Up First

Don't buy more of something before you use what you have on hand—for example: fabric, wrapping paper, and stationery.

Easy Fix

Baking soda down the drain is an easy freshener;
and baking soda with vinegar is a frugal drain cleaner.

Limited Wheels

One car per driver over age eighteen is plenty
for a family to maintain.

Plan for Emergencies

Have a set plan for emergencies.
Create a portable emergency kit that you
can grab and take with you. Pack a large
kit of supplies for surviving a long period of
time without electricity and other utilities.

Baking
Choose home-baked cookies and cakes over bakery or prepackaged—you control the ingredients and the cost.

Clutter-Free

A cluttered environment mirrors a cluttered mind.
Clean and organize your environment,
and you will be surprised at how much
more clearly you are able to think.

Gardening

Plant and tend a garden—whether big or small.
Gardening slows you down, relaxes you,
and makes you appreciate the cycle of life.

{ File It or Lose It

Keep all papers filed in organized folders.
Set aside a regular time for tucking the
papers away so that your desk and
tables stay clear. }

Less Is More—Collections

If you collect something, make it one thing,
and give it a special place in your house
where it can have purpose and meaning.

Manners Matter

Teach your children proper manners and practice them daily in the home as well as in public.

United Calendar
Consolidate all family members' activities onto one calendar.

{

Be Uncommon

When you do the common things in life
in an uncommon way, you will
command the attention of the world.
GEORGE WASHINGTON CARVER

}

Welcome Change

Change opens us to new possibilities, new experiences,
new lessons in life. So celebrate the changes
that come your way and go with the flow.

Be Creative

Do something each week that is a creative outlet.
Celebrate your accomplishment.

Buddy System

Two are better than one, because they have a
good return for their work: If one falls down,
his friend can help him up. But pity the man
who falls and has no one to help him up!

ECCLESIASTES 4:9–10 NIV

{

Family Tree

Keep in touch with your extended family.
Know where you came from and appreciate
the family legacy you have.
Whether common or legendary, we
can all learn from our ancestors.

}

Bloom Where You Are Planted

Be content with what you have and make the
most of what you have at any given time.
If you are always waiting for bigger and better,
you'll miss the blessings of the present.

Always on Time

Give yourself an extra fifteen minutes to get to your destination so you are never late. But, if you find yourself running late, have the courtesy to call ahead.

Prioritize

Make a list of your overall life priorities and feel free to say "no" to anything that does not align with those priorities.

Stamp Out Problems

Deal with conflicts early, before they grow into real problems. But if someone or something is a continual annoyance, avoid it and focus on something more positive.

Sleep
A regular full night's sleep is required for recharging the body.

Quality over Quantity

Choose quality over quantity. You can fill your home
with lots of cheap junk that won't last a year,
but your money is better spent on one item of quality
that will be useful for years to come.

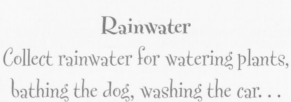

Rainwater
Collect rainwater for watering plants,
bathing the dog, washing the car. . .

Downsizing Space

Consider downsizing your home. It reduces your belongings to only what you need, as well as reduces your living costs.

Online Bill Paying
Pay your bills through your bank's online system
to save time and money.

Prayerful Choices

Pray before making decisions. Even seemingly small choices can affect the direction of your whole life.

Be an Example

Children learn best by example—no fancy teaching plans needed if you are living to the best of your potential in front of your children.

{

Memories

Creating a memory doesn't
have to cost a dime.

}

Be a Good Citizen
Know your rights, appreciate your freedoms,
and strive to protect them.

Respect God

He who fears the LORD has a secure fortress,
and for his children it will be a refuge.
PROVERBS 14:26 NIV

Fully Present
Be fully present in each moment of life
so you are fully engaged in your relationships.
Avoid multitasking, especially in social settings.

Routines

Kids thrive on the comforts of having a routine, so establish daily family routines they can count on.

Sacred Home

Don't bring anything into your home that you don't want to have influence over your family. Carefully monitor time with TV, Internet, and other media influences. Likewise, don't bring home the stresses of work that can pollute your attitude and spoil your family time.

Take a Break

If something seems hard or continually frustrating, take a break from it. Be it a small project or a weekly commitment, step back from it, and when you return, it should look more achievable.

Truth

Define what *truth* is for you within the context of
your faith and live within truth's boundaries.
If you do, you'll learn there are fewer
gray areas in life than you thought.

Get Some Sunshine

Don't hide from the sun. Daily time spent outdoors in indirect sunlight is good for the body. (Be sure to use sunscreen!)

Get Back Time

Look for things you feel are time wasters—those things that should only take minutes but quickly add up to hours and make you feel guilty for the time that has been lost. Perhaps it is TV or Internet time. Maybe it's your commute to and from work. Find ways to eliminate or control any wasted time.

Verbalize

Know what's important to you and voice your priorities. Don't expect others to read your mind. We waste a lot of energy and emotion on unspoken feelings that never get resolved. So talk it out.

Family Kitchen
Involve the whole family in preparing
a meal and doing the cleanup.

Be a Teacher

Take responsibility for teaching your children everything they need to be fully rounded adults. First and foremost, prepare their spiritual lives because this will have eternal ramifications. Be involved in their educational training. Help them with choosing the things that will best shape their social lives. Know their friends.

God's Portion

Return to God a portion of all He gives you
(time, money, and more), and trust Him
to provide for all your needs.

Preserve

Buy bulk fruits and vegetables grown locally in season and preserve them yourself by canning, freezing, and drying for wholesome year-round use.

Spending Doesn't Buy Happiness
More things and new things don't always equal better things. You don't need every new gadget on the market. The joy you feel when first getting something you want quickly fades.

Recycle

Recycle your trash, and recycle
old things to new life.

Wisdom

For wisdom is better than rubies; and all the things
that may be desired are not to be compared to it.

PROVERBS 8:11 KJV

Raise Chickens

A small backyard flock of chickens or ducks gives you multiple returns: eggs, the potential for meat, and hours of relaxing fun watching the birds' antics.

Simple Funnel and Bucket
Reuse milk jugs by cutting the tops off for funnels
and using the lower part with the handle
for a bucket.

{

Limit Gifts

Set the rule to only give the kids "free"
toys on Christmas and birthdays.
Teach them to save for and buy their
own wants the rest of the year.

}

Be Active

Stay physically active, and include your children in your walks, swims, biking, and other activites.

Prep Ahead

Prepare the night before by setting out breakfast food,
packing lunches, putting supper in the slow cooker,
and so on to avoid the morning rush.

Sing a Song

Sing while alone to make your work more enjoyable.
Sing together as a family the songs of faith
to reinforce what you believe and silly songs
to help everyone relax.

Pick One Activity

Have your children pick one activity outside their schoolwork and home life to be devoted to (be it a sport, a musical instrument, a club, etc.). Let it be just one thing that they will take lessons for and practice during the week. The less children are involved in, the more time there is for giving their best to the activity of their choice and not end up hurting their schoolwork and family time.

Satisfaction

Laziness may appear attractive,
but work gives satisfaction.

ANNE FRANK

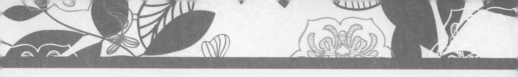

Answered Prayer

Acknowledge answered prayers. Doing so will encourage faith in your kids, your spouse, your friends, and yourself. Celebrate God's answer, even if it wasn't what you wanted or expected.

A Yard That Works

Turn a wasted area of your yard into a garden that produces food for your table. Plant shrubs like blueberries that give you a sweet return. Choose an apple tree to shade a corner of your lawn and reap the added benefits of fruit.

{

Weekly Menu

Plan a week of meals ahead and be sure
you have all the ingredients on hand.
Then deciding what to make for dinner
becomes a breeze.

}

Know History
Know historical facts and strive not to
repeat the disgraceful parts.

Joy Stock

Make an effort at least once a week to list things
to be thankful and joyful for. The more you focus
on these blessings the less time you will have
for negative thoughts and attitudes.

Free to Be
Focus on doing things together with your family
and friends that are free—a hike, a backyard
game, camping, star-gazing. . .

Don't Worry

{ "Therefore I tell you, do not worry about your life, what you will eat or drink; or about your body, what you will wear. Is not life more important than food, and the body more important than clothes? Look at the birds of the air; they do not sow or reap or store away in barns, and yet your heavenly Father feeds them. Are you not much more valuable than they? Who of you by worrying can add a single hour to his life?" }

MATTHEW 6:25-27 NIV

Time-Out

Take a time-out midday. Leave your desk for lunch.
Take a power nap. Take a walk.

No-Chatter Zone

Limit your time in idle chatter, especially in things like texting, Twittering, forums, blogs, and the like.
Set up safety zones where no electronic chatter will be allowed—like no texting during dinner and no instant messaging while at work. Instead, spend more time and effort in communicating with others face-to-face.

Forgive

Always be willing to forgive—and to accept forgiveness. True peace comes only when we can face our mistakes and be reconciled with others in our lives.

{

Self-Sufficient

Learn a skill that can help you better provide for your family—bread baking, cheese making, sewing, plumbing. . .

}

Simply Clean

A simple solution of one part vinegar and four parts water will wash windows, countertops, and more.

Family Devotions

Participate in devotional readings and
discussions together as a family.

Talk About It

Regular communication wards off
many problems in the home.

{

Front Porch Swing

Sit on your porch awhile each day.
Listen to the frogs. Watch the fireflies.
Feed the hummingbirds.

}

Find Purpose

Prayerfully determine your purpose in life, then before you add anything to your life (be it a thing or an activity), decide if it aligns with your purpose. If not, discard it.

A Family Affair

Make household projects family fun and learning times. Listen to an audio book while doing dishes. Play a game like twenty questions while pulling weeds. Talk to the children about their dreams while painting.

Don't Overbook

Don't book appointments and other things you do back-to-back. Give yourself breathing room in between.

Don't Get Trapped

Gossip is like quicksand. Don't let yourself get caught up in idle conversation—whether true or not—that only leads to hurt and pain.

Double Up
Double or triple a recipe and freeze the extra portions for quick future meals.

Lighten Your Load

Carry only what is absolutely necessary
in your purse, wallet, car, gym bag. . .

Be Generous

One man gives freely, yet gains even more;
another withholds unduly, but comes to poverty.

PROVERBS 11:24 NIV

Your Favorite Hobby

Pick one hobby you are passionate about
and focus your energy on it instead of
spreading your time and energy over
multiple interests you can't fully
devote yourself to.

A Place for Everything

Everything should have its place and be returned there after use. Set aside the half-hour before bedtime to go around and look for anything that has been left out of place.

What's Enough?

Learn what having "enough" really means to you—
enough money, enough things, enough time—
and be content to stop at "enough."

Puzzles

Work a puzzle together as a family. It can be relaxing, as well as teach cooperation and patience.

Wash and Wear

Buy clothes that are easy to wash and wear.
Buy them in coordinating colors for many
mix-and-match options.

Credit Card Downsize
Pay off and destroy all credit cards except
one that you keep paid off each month.

Backyard Foods

Forage some food from your own backyard—
dandelion greens, wild berries, etc.

Be Firm

Stand firm in your beliefs and convictions.

Family Dinner

Eat at least one meal a day together as a family. Use the time for each person to discuss things that are important in their life.

Money Managers
Work with your children and teach
them to be good managers of money.

Time to Be a Kid

Keep your children's schedules simple.
Don't let their time be overloaded.
Allow them time to play and just be kids.

Appreciate a Sunrise

Wake up early enough to see and enjoy the sunrise.
Ponder how each day is a new beginning,
a chance to begin afresh.

Absorb a Sunset

Slow down to admire sunsets.
Consider how all things must rest each day
and take it to heart.

Homemade Is Better

Give homemade items as gifts—jams, knitted scarves, photos, and the like—instead of pricey things shipped in from overseas.

Be Resourceful

Lazy people don't even cook the game they catch,
but the diligent make use of everything they find.
PROVERBS 12:27 NLT

Simple Style

Maintain a hairstyle that is easy to fix each morning and inexpensive to maintain. High hair salon bills are often a drain on a family budget.

Safety Net

Start a savings account and put aside what you would need to live on for at least three months if your income should be severed.

Fewer Choices
Variety can add clutter, so don't stock more than two varieties of things like tea bags, cereal, shampoo, etc.

Kids Are Teachable

Teach kids to do many things for themselves as soon as
they are reasonably able. Give them each a chore
to be responsible for and start them in small steps
along the path to independence.

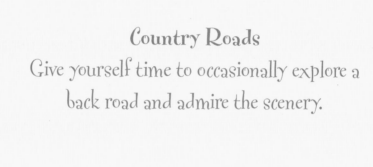

Country Roads

Give yourself time to occasionally explore a
back road and admire the scenery.

Know Your Neighbors

Create a network among neighbors so you can call on someone close if you should have a problem.

Timed Reminders
Set a timer to remind the family to start getting ready so you'll always be on time.

Seeds for Life

Use heirloom seeds in your garden that can be
saved from year to year, preserving traditional
varieties and saving you money.

To Love a Pet

Don't add a pet to the household until you calculate
the lifetime cost, have a primary caregiver,
and know who will care for it when
you inevitably have to be away.

Build a Haven

Make your home a safe haven for your children and their friends.

Group Hobby

Find a hobby or activity the whole family can participate in together on a regular basis.

Know Your Food Sources

Know where your food comes from and know how to provide wholesome food for your table. Buy and eat the majority of your food grown locally.

Friends
Accept offers of friendship
and be a friend in return.

{

Compost

Compost your yard waste and
kitchen scraps into new dirt.

}

Seek Rest

"Come to me, all you who are weary and burdened,
and I will give you rest."

MATTHEW 11:28 NIV

Don't Be Influenced

Don't let what others have influence your ideas of
what things are truly necessary or needed.

Save Together
Have a savings goal the whole family
can work toward together.

Scheduled Time

Block out regular family time on the weekly
calendar and don't let anything else take
precedence.

Stop the Madness

Refuse to run yourself ragged trying to get done those
little things that have a way of either getting done
themselves, not mattering in the big picture,
or that can wait until another time.

On the Bright Side

Try to see the positive side of every situation.

Rag Bag

An old T-shirt rag will last one hundred times
longer and preserve more trees and money
than buying paper towels each week.
Start a rag bag from old clothes and towels
instead of throwing them away.

Simply Ordinary

The ordinary arts we practice every day
at home are of more importance to the
soul than their simplicity might suggest.
THOMAS MORE

Siesta
Take a midafternoon break for the health
of your mind and body.

Do You Really Need It?

Don't be a slave to clever marketing. Even the best sale may not be on an item you really need.

Be Honest
Don't do anything that you know will
make you feel guilty later.

Avoid Temptations

Stay away from those things that cause you to only want more than you need in any given area of life. Choose instead to protect your sensibilities.

Recycled Containers

Food containers from things like yogurt, sour cream, margarine, and more can have extended life as containers for leftovers and freezing food.

Volunteer

Make an effort to volunteer to help those less fortunate through things like a church pantry, a homeless shelter, Habitat for Humanity, and the like.

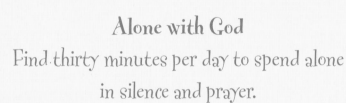

Alone with God

Find thirty minutes per day to spend alone
in silence and prayer.

Keep No Debt

Owe no man any thing,
but to love one another.
ROMANS 13:8 KJV

Front Porch Chat

Take a Sunday afternoon to visit a neighbor
on the front porch.

Stay on Task

Stay with one task at a time and don't get distracted by trying to multitask. Thoroughly complete the first item on your "to-do" list before moving on to the next.

Food for Health
Eat your food as close to its natural state
as possible. Say no to processed foods
with many preservatives.

Fall Behind

Give yourself permission not to keep
up with every new fad. It is okay to
let your style fall out of date
or your car to lose its luster.

Libraries Are Treasures
Use your local library—saves money and keeps your home library limited to only those books that are ultimate favorites.

Don't Hoard

Don't keep things that you no longer use or will never need. Since use of clothing is hard to track, tag each garment when you bring clothes out for a new season. Remove the tag when you wear it. At the end of the season, don't return to storage anything still wearing its tag.

Blackout

Do voluntary power downs for a portion of each day and rely only on manual power. It will help you to 1) save money, 2) slow down, and 3) be more appreciative. In fact, a family night spent with only light from oil lamp, candles, and a fireplace can be quite fun for all.

Sit by a Bonfire

There is something about fire that draws us
and comforts us. Being out under the stars
and surrounded by nature is relaxing.
There is also something strangely liberating
in the experience of cooking our food
over open flames.

End of Season Bargains
Plan ahead and buy things you need at the end
of a season when items are discounted.

Reduction

Reduce the complexity of life by eliminating
the needless wants of life, and the labors
of life reduce themselves.
EDWIN WAY TEALE

Trash It

Don't open junk mail. Don't save tempting catalogs filled with things you don't need. Send them directly to the trash.

Timing

Know when is the best time for you and your family members to make big decisions. Avoid conflicts by avoiding focused discussions during distractions, times of fatigue, periods of stress, and the like.

Classic Gems

Dig into classic literature and art, and find
treasures that hearken back to simpler times.

Harness Nature

Find simple ways to use the power of the wind, the sun, and water in your work and home.

Plan Ahead

In the house of the wise are stores of choice food
and oil, but a foolish man devours all he has.

PROVERBS 21:20 NIV

Loved

The supreme happiness in life is the
conviction that we are loved—loved
for ourselves, or rather, loved in
spite of ourselves.
Victor Hugo

Ice Bottles
Freeze bottles of water to use as cooler ice packs and as dead-space filler to make your freezer run more efficiently.

Baking for Bonding

Family members bond over things like baking cookies together. As a plus, kitchen skills are learned and good food is the reward.

Off-Season

Book vacation travel during off-seasons for huge savings. Airlines, hotels, parks, and more offer great deals to entice travelers when bookings are generally low.

Read a Book

Turn off the TV and read more books.
Try reading a book together as a
family and discussing the story.

Tote Along Food

Avoid convenience-food traps while traveling
and pack a cooler full of wholesome snacks.

Out of the Way

When faced with many necessary tasks in a day, choose to do the hardest ones first so that your load gets lighter as the list gets shorter.

Know Your Limits

Have a good idea of how much your body and mind can take. Take a break before you become overexerted and overstressed.

Principles

In matters of principle, stand like a rock.
THOMAS JEFFERSON

Define *Simple*

Write down what a simplified life for you would look like. Start eliminating things that don't fit into that picture. Then when faced with a decision, ask what the simplified version of you would do.